THE HERE AND NOW OF IT

Poems by David Connor

BLUE LIGHT PRESS ◆ 1ST WORLD PUBLISHING

1ˢᵗ WORLD
PUBLISHING

SAN FRANCISCO ◆ FAIRFIELD ◆ DELHI

The Here and Now of It

Copyright ©2017 by David Connor

1st World Library
PO Box 2211
Fairfield, IA 52556
www.1stworldpublishing.com

Blue Light Press
www.bluelightpress.com
Email: bluelightpress@aol.com

Book & Cover Design
Melanie Gendron
www.melaniegendron.com

First Edition
ISBN 978-1-4218-3789-5
Library of Congress Control Number: 2017954679

THE HERE AND NOW OF IT

TABLE OF CONTENTS

I.   DOGS AT THE BEACH

II.   ABRAHAM'S CHILDREN

III.   HOME DELIVERY

IV.   COURTING AT THE STRAWBERRY

I. DOGS AT THE BEACH

DOGS AT THE BEACH

Along the pebbled beach
I walked my two dogs,
elderly Bichon Frises, pure white,
near remains of the Quan family home
who, in their day, 100 years ago,
caught and sun-dried brine shrimp
from the smooth shallow bay
which still defines China Camp.

A grey mist rising,
shading the horizon,
melded into scattered clouds,
which allowed patches
of an azure sky to calm our nerves.

I imagined nets filled with crustacea
hauled over gunnels of small fishing skiffs
with back muscles straining until boats were laden.

They saved the fat ones for Fisherman's Wharf
and hungry tourist appetites,
while bundles of dried and salted shrimp
were loaded and sent on the long ocean voyage
to eager Chinese patrons in sophisticated diners,
hungrily consuming delicacies from California.

Dogs have an excellent olfactory sense.
They sniffed around the old drying racks,
and as they inhaled aromas from the past,
looked lovingly at me with yearnings for shrimp.

A MARCH EVENING

A cold mist crept over the shoreline
off Humboldt Bay in Eureka,
where the estuary of the Elk River
once fed native tribes.

Huddled beneath the eaves
of the locked public restroom,
a pair of homeless, shivering adults
asked for assistance.

I go prepared when I wander at night
by wearing boots, woolen pants
and a hooded jacket, but I also
carry a pack of unopened cigarettes
and 2 five dollar bills, which I handed over.

They were grateful and asked,
"What can we give you?"
I said, "You just did by accepting my gift."

AFTER A DAY OF BOCCE

Bocce is a bowling game
invented by the French,
popularized by Italians
and played on American courts.
Bowling a bocce with friends
eases the mind and fortifies the spirit.

Forget about the winds and tides.
Concentrate on sun, stance and release.
As you send your ball towards the target,
troubles from the day evaporate.
Thoughts buzzing like a swarm of bees
will disappear when you find the Queen's hive.

With a Bocce game tied at 10,
you have the small white ball to set the point,
aim for the 60 foot mark and leave
the target 18 inches from the sideboard
so the other team will wonder about your strategy.

What was Wordsworth thinking
when he praised nature and daffodils?
Where was Frost leading us
when he decided on the road less traveled?
How did Hardy bow to a dying thrush,
and why did Byron find such majesty
in the endless repetition of a rolling ocean?

I have possessed magical elements
that dreams and prayers are made of
but only need the love of an old dog,
a quiet hour of bocce ball on oyster shells,
and a cup so small it is always overflowing.

LUNAR ECLIPSE

Today's shadow slipped silently
over the full moon's glistening face,
mixing light with dark as we unburdened ourselves
with quietude in worshipful tones.

I could have been a man of fortune,
living alone on an island retreat but awash in gloom,
since there is no future when you have plucked
juicy grapes from last years vintage.

Better to sleep soundly with today's memories
than to wish for a better tomorrow.
There will be no lunar eclipse in the eastern sky
to welcome you to your morning.

THE RIDE DOWN

*"Life is reaching the top of the hill
and enjoying the ride down."*
—James Taylor

At age 18 I put my hiking boots on,
climbed to the peak of the Thunder Bay Range,
walked the rim around Yosemite
and stood at the top of Half Dome.
On the summit of Stow Mountain's ski run,
I closed my eyes and swooshed down the slope.

Alone on a day with a clear view of billowing clouds,
I loved riding in a gondola, swept on tiny cables
over Heavenly Valley and Lake Tahoe.

After a long evening of Madeira banqueting,
I was relieved after sliding down a twisting road
at Funchal in a sled, to step off intact.

As I grow old, I'm running out of mountains to climb,
risks to challenge me, and discomforts to endure.
Job opportunities are becoming scarce, but I'm content
to slumber well while dreaming of submerged caves I've entered.
Then, as I slip up from sleepy ocean dreams,
I'm ready to face another day in my valley.

FISHING ON HUMBOLDT BAY

Krill are the smallest edible objects
that herd up and are swallowed
by animals larger and higher up the food chain.

Whales gulp tons of krill to grow.
Salmon gorge while waiting to spawn.
White gulls scoop them, small fish smell them.
All are happy with their living meals.

The not so azure overcast sky
covered a barely creased green sea
from which we reeled in 30 pound King Salmons
while showered with spray from blue whales.

Our 24 foot boat was loaded with fish
whose intestines were stuffed with krill.
They were competing in a feeding frenzy
with the pod of rising whales off our stern.

Although we invaded their territory,
the whales didn't seem to mind.
They were here first, prompt for lunch,
and several times our size.

Whale droppings fertilize the ocean bottom,
but krill poop doesn't have time to drop.
Human waste will have to wait
until a steaming salmon is devoured.

People, whales, birds and salmon
had a fine day of fishing on Humboldt Bay.
Only the krill thought differently.

TO MY DOG BELLA

Your teeny weeny bladder
has a teeny weeny cancer,
and your bleeding is spotting the rugs.
Good thing you're an old arthritic dog,
so we can put you to sleep
when your suffering becomes too much.

If you were an old man,
we'd get permission from Medicare
to do a PET scan, and if negative,
perform a radical cystectomy.
You'd be trundled off to a nursing home
since your ureteral stents would drain into a bag.

Smelling like rotten fish, complaining
of aches, pains, a poor appetite
and how you cannot defecate or sleep,
you'd be nasty to your grandkids.
Since you had no money,
no one would visit or send cards.

Sharing a room with three old men
who are demented, drooling
and suffering through daytime TV,
you'd forget to thank the nursing aides
who puff your pillow and give you baths.
You would only think of your suffering,
with no one feeling sorry for you.

Too bad we can't treat a man like a dog
and just say goodbye, it's been a good life.

SAN FRANCISCO SHORE

Whales are washing ashore
from Half Moon Bay to Alcatraz.
The Oakland Bay Bridge,
recently built since it fell apart
during the earthquake of 1989,
has now sprung several salty leaks.

Elsewhere, the Colorado River cannot flood
Lake Mead behind Hoover Dam.
Our drought continues.
Lettuce and strawberries are wilting,
but people still fill pools and water lawns
while waiting for the next wildfire
spread by Santa Ana winds.

I want to protect the shores of the world,
and keep them clean and free.
I feel for the oily birds and injured seals.
I want all fish to have a clean habitat
to mate, spawn, swim in the ocean
and come back to the rivers
without being covered with debris.

I'll go to Baker Beach, view the bridge
and walk the surf in bare feet,
wishing for rain so I can fish
for fat steelhead trout, females full of egg sacs,
still off shore waiting for the river's mouth to open
so they can swim upstream and escape
the hungry seals who eat only the mothers.

RIVER TROUBADOUR

In a canoe on the Chetko River in British Columbia,
I was thinking a poem.
I was bow, my host stern.
I was all image; he was narrative.

We trailed a fishing line
as an epigram for a hungry rainbow trout.
The river dragged us along
as if we were being towed.
The canoe had a beginning,
bulged in the middle,
with a meaningful ending.
Words fell like snow from willows.
We netted some of them,
and the fish ate the rest.

We stopped to cast lines
towards expanding ripples,
saw words and fish rise
as our lines ran together.

Around the campfire, I recited the poem
like a French trapper turned troubadour.
A pileated woodpecker pecked the rhythm,
and a golden crowned thrush applauded.

WALKING IN THE TRINITY FOREST

I love being a male in the Trinity forest,
without fear of bears and able to pee on trees.
I love hockey, human collisions on ice,
but was not very good at football or lacrosse.
I am not a seamstress but can assist
sewing body parts back onto patients.
I love to eat animals I hunt or catch,
but am not a killer of anything else.
I never fired a bullet during my tour of duty,
but I am not a pacifist.

I am a poet but will never be as gifted as
Seamus Heaney, Elinor Wylie or Wallace Stevens.
I was father to three daughters and have camped out
with the youngest in Yosemite Valley.

I am in love with the dark
and wander at night without a light
since there are floating wraiths
who need an audience but won't come near
since they might not yet be dead.

KIDS AND DOGS

I walk my two Bichon Frises at dawn
if they are awake, fed, and approve
of the local weather conditions,
since rain and cold bother their arthritis.
We walk the path around a lagoon
hoping to encounter other dogs.

Only dogs walk with leashes;
cats and peacocks don't.
Coming upon a strange new canine,
Bitsy sniffs and is friendly
while Bella, her sister, growls and bares teeth.

Not all dogs or kids are created equal;
social and income inequalities begin at birth.
Some are born to be rich;
others have to learn not to growl.

GRIM REAPER

I feel more evil than Iago or Macbeth
and shameful enough to make confession
as I wait to hand my ancient dogs over
to the veterinarian for euthanasia.

Both are now older in body than humans,
who are usually drooling in nursing homes
because their next of kin avoids responsibility
for dealing with diseases or disposable diapers.

As adults we should be happy to have lived
so many years that we stand to suffer
the ravages of dementia and incontinence
with a steady demand to turn the volume up.

My dogs still radiate uncompromising love,
which doesn't offset inappropriate behavior
around the house. Despite arthritic joints,
they're always begging for another walk,
dishes with small bites of lamb and rice,
and sleeping in our bed.

Farmers love their animals
and make friends with chickens, sheep, pigs and koi
before killing and eating them.
Dogs fall into the category of friend, not food.
I'll miss their licks, snuggles and adoring glances
but not the soiled carpets which eased them to heaven,
where I can see them nightly with the Gemini twins.

MESSAGE FROM DOG HEAVEN

My dogs went to doggie heaven
and reported back through the Seraph
specializing in Bichons newly arrived.
I could hear from their hearts and souls
a language we all understood.

They are in the denial stage;
it happened so quickly.
Earlier that day the three of us
were cuddled about my lap
in a poolside chair flooded with sun.

At the Vet's they were stripped naked,
collars and leashes handed back.
Their recently groomed tails waved goodbye
as they rounded the corner heading to doom.

Now, in their heaven, they are angry and bargaining
for a reprieve and a chance to treat carpets better.
They are aching for a walk around the boats
and doggie biscuit treats from their master.

They recall the good times we had together:
the ride in the Petco cart sniffing cat food,
strolls on the wrack at China Camp,
walks in the rain at Montecito Plaza,
rides in the truck to Albert and Peacock parks
to watch big dogs and little kids play.

St. Peter remembered Tasia,
the owner's pet with kidney failure.
She showed up 13 years ago and wonders if they had met?
No, they said. We were only the replacements.

VISIONS OF PEACE

Was the first moment you grieved
the time you buried your dog?
Did your heart ache in the morning
as you woke up without him?

I often sat alone on the limb
of an apple tree near his fresh grave.
Dense woods begged exploration,
but without my companion
I feared the unknown.

To signal the end of my adolescence,
I leapt through a fire before 6000 people.
I remember the final whistle ending
my last school hockey game.
Ten years later, I stepped ashore
from my final cruise on the USS Sperry
where I lived for a year.

As I turned thirty, a six year marriage
ended without fanfare
and my amateur fishing career began.
I learned if I didn't catch a fish today,
there will be more waiting in the morning.

I will never again march in full uniform
during an anti-war peace parade,
but I agree with the convictions
of McGovern, Stafford and King
that we need peace without victory.

Though I have lived eight decades
within a country usually at conflict,
I have lived a life of peace at home.
I hope my children will never be drafted
or have to read about the ravages of war.

A BIT OF A POEM ABOUT A BIT OF INK

The period is the smallest thing
in a sentence, except for the dot
over a lower case "i" in Font 8.

Large, open periods are gaudy
and look like a filled in "O"
especially on the cheer sweaters
of 16-year-old coeds with perky breasts.

A vertical line over a period
makes it an exclamation point,
especially when mad or vexed.
Long periods can become ages,
but when you're alive,
historians haven't decided
what age you're living in
or what it will be called.

My sister came to breakfast and announced
she hadn't had a period for two months.
My mother fainted,
my father threw up in his oatmeal
and I, only 10, wondered
how she could ever finish a sentence without a period?

Sections of a hockey game are called periods
and vary in length from 12 minutes in pee-wees
to 15 in high school and 20 in college and the pros.
20 was the number of teeth remaining in the mouth
of Gump Worsley of the Detroit Red Wings
when he retired as the best of goalies in the NHL.

Whenever mother got mad, she stamped her foot
and yelled, "Come, Here, Now, Period."
Maybe she was still looking for
the period my sister lost.

DUCK CALL

My friend and I are in the blind,
crouched down so ducks won't see us
as we're clothed in camouflage
and silent in a sunken pit.

We're surrounded by buoyant model ducks
in the Butte Sink near Colusa,
with a spirited, trembling young black lab
waiting for the first morning shot.

Four cock sprigs zero in on the decoys,
spread their wings for descent.
Joe shoots the two on the left,
I get both on the right
and the dog retrieves all four
to his delight and our praise
as the sun rises over the pond.

This is living in the full possibility
of the moment we are sharing:
three happy hunters,
four dead ducks,
a wave of mallards approaching,
meaning fine eats and plenty left over.

II. ABRAHAM'S CHILDREN

ABRAHAM'S CHILDREN

My wife and I visited Abraham's tomb
shortly after worshipers were massacred.
We heard a bomb in Hebron as we exited our bus
in a land where all pay lip service
to Abraham as father to us all.

Abraham was sire to future generations
whose current descendants are at war
with each other and the world
after the Twin Towers collapsed,
leaving unnumbered corpses in rubble.

Our tour group entered Jerusalem
from the side of Mt. Nemo
after paying homage to the tomb of Moses.
We were guided through narrow streets
around churches, mosques and temples.
We thought if people can worship together,
they should be able to live in harmony.

As we were standing on steps to a mosque
and posing for a romantic camera shot,
a gardner approached and chastised us
for holding hands and kissing.

If marital bliss is illegal
why can't they outlaw war?

MR. HUDSON

His gapped tooth smile
surrounded by a handsome black face,
is broad, ready and welcoming
with healthy appreciation for the help he needs
and receives from attentive medical staff.

By profession, a chef in New York City
with a list of famous restaurants to his claim.
Now, burdened with a terminal kidney illness,
his cooking days are over.
He is now the customer at the table
where I am the attending server.

We talk about poetry. He has a hidden love
for the printed word, and worships Elizabethan times
and Shakespearean language in plays and poetry.
He recites Jaques' "All the world's a stage" for me;
I give him a signed copy of my book.

By the following week, we speak in current terms,
leaving the forsooths and harken thees behind.
I share what I was thinking
when writing about my dogs.

He has the dignity and strength of the brave,
the tolerance and patience of a saint
and a likability I envy in the disabled.
My hope for him is a kidney transplant,
but we both know that his joy
would have to come from another's sorrow.

A DAY AT THE POOL

My two year Navy tour in the '60s
taught me to never volunteer for duty,
but today I raised my hand
to take my friend's daughter, age 6,
to the Rolling Hills swimming pool,
as the Marin flatlands were scorched.

A grandmother was on the next chaise
tending to her 2-year-old, who couldn't swim.
When I tired of losing lap races
to my 6-year-old charge, we rested.

The elderly neighbor asked questions,
which my tadpole promptly answered:

>   "My mom and dad run a restaurant.
>   She cooks and laughs; he's the waiter."
>
>   "It's called Beso's Bistro and it's at Hamilton Field."
>
>   "They have a very full menu,
>   and the selections are all good."
>
>   "I like the tender chicken best."

After more swimming we returned to our chair,
but it was covered with someone's clothes.
I moved them to the next chaise, which was empty,
and was insulted by a very large man
who strutted over and demanded
we move everything back in place.

My little sweet talking girl
picked up her shoes and towel
and quietly nudged me towards the exit
to avoid further dealings and troubles
with that massive weapon of destruction.

We went home and walked her dogs.
Sammy and Jesse were delighted to see us.
I believe this 6 year old will win
a Nobel Prize for Peace and Diplomacy.

IT'S A COYOTE'S WORLD

"we plant nothing, yet harvest it all
you see, it never occurred to ever leave Eden"
"Coyote Meditation" by Dale Biron
From *Why We Do Our Daily Practices*

Movements of the heavenly bodies
were a mystery to the ancients
until they gave them names.

Sirius looks like a dog sniffing a hunter.
We root for Orion and his bow and arrow
to pierce Aldeberon, the nose of Taurus, the bull.

The Gemini twins likely had a contagious disease
as they were shuttled away from important constellations.
The best job for the Big Dipper was to point North
so sailors wouldn't fall off the edge of the earth.

Animals are born able to walk,
needing neither clothes nor shelter.
They survive by foraging, hunting or fishing,
and never start wars.

When humans invaded animal territory,
their homes took up natural space once reserved
by the creatures who now tip over garbage cans,
tear camping trailers apart, and eat small domestic pets.

Our neighborhood pack of coyotes lived here
before I made enough money to buy a house in their woods.
I enjoy their howls and squeals when they find food
and enjoy their heaven on earth.

There was never a Coyote constellation,
so they must have bothered the ancients.

AT THE MELBOURNE FISH MARKET

Large green eels are sold alive
at the Melbourne fish market,
where you can select the creature from a tank.
The fishmonger yanks it from the water,
weighs it, kills it, guts it,
and you take it home to cook it.

Customers want to see
the freshness and muscularity
of the slippery, squirming fish
before they make their purchase
for the family dinner.

A 20 pound, 4 foot specimen from hell
wanted nothing to do with the scales.
He flipped and broke the grasp,
flopped three times on the sawdust floor
while the lady with the money
encouraged the handler to hurry,
weigh it, and hand it over.

Finally, the proprietor won the battle
by bashing in the brains of the fighter
with a ball-peen hammer and piercing its eyes
with a sharpened screwdriver.
Before placing it back on the scale,
he drove a long spike through the sockets
for better handling on the voyage home.

The fussy lady objected
as she wanted a living, gulping eel.
She said her husband would have a fit
if she didn't deliver their meal alive.

"Lady, this is your eel.
You picked it, I packed it.
Send your husband next time
and I'll let him pick the eel he wants.
I'll put them both in the same tank of water,
without weapons and see who wins."

ANOTHER DRIVER HEARD FROM

My daughter and I abhor
a front seat passenger suggesting
with fidgeting nervous twitches
that the driver doesn't have a clue
how to propel a vehicle.

I know what STOP means,
can see an octagon from 100 feet,
have unsighted knowledge of the brake pad
and know the 2nd derivative of moving objects.
I don't need sweaty palms on the elbow rest
to remind me I'm approaching Dante's circles.

I also expect the driver who starts
the engine and buckles up
to know the destination.

One sunny Sunday morning in April,
with Mission Bay's early fog abating,
she decided to drive.
As we set out for the San Diego Aquarium,
she missed a sign around La Jolla
and didn't see an obscure turnoff.

We were lost but agreed to recover by returning
to the Dana Spa and Resort swimming pool
to cool off, find a more detailed map,
and complete our adventure.

We met the Octopus related to Inky,
who had wiggled through a drain pipe
and escaped to the ocean from the LA Zoo.
We reached into a tide pool,
squeezed slimy things,
saw schools of coral fish over fields of sand dabs,
and kept our distance from barracuda and sharks.

Hugs, kisses and reassurances
from my daughter assured me
that despite domestic troubles,
we can find our direction together.

HEAVEN'S SPY

The first time I saw a daddy-long-legs
was on a spring morning at Lake Harriet, Minneapolis.
I was scooping up water for my goldfish.
It was standing on some twigs
and had legs so thin
they looked like pins in the cushion
on my mother's Singer sewing machine.

The spider looked too frail to be dangerous,
unlike the tarantula we saw at a school assembly.
I could have squashed it with my Keds size 8 shoe
but didn't because it was just wandering around,
moving on its spindly legs
from twig to twig.

It seemed to be aware of everything about me
so I guessed it was God
keeping track of His creations,
watching me bring fresh water home
for the two goldfish I won
at the Baptist Youth Bible Verse Bee.

The eighth grade girl who came in first
won two ballpoint pens,
which leaked and ruined her dress.
My goldfish lasted 5 years
and had a proper burial
12 inches deep in the garden
below my bedroom window.
Their coffin was two Kerr zinc canning lids
sealed with Mystic tape.

MY FIRST CAMPING TRIP

I hated it when the tent leaked
and I had to put on wet underwear
after spending the night swatting bugs
and listening to a hoot owl.

I disliked the cold cocoa and hot lemonade
and got annoyed when the fishing line broke.
We had to let the trout go free,
so we ate spam and onions for dinner.

We found an abandoned miner's cabin
and ran like little goats for shelter,
but there wasn't much of a roof,
and it leaked all night into buckets.

The next morning our canoe hit a rock
and sprung a leak. We got soaked
pulling it to shore to patch the canvas
so we could paddle through rapids.

The poison ivy wasn't bad
until we had to use the latrine.
Bears and raccoons stole our food,
so we ate our last candy bars.

When I got home and unpacked,
my Mom asked me about the woods.
I told her we had a wonderful time.

ON THE CLOCK

Farmers and fishermen are like animals —
neither are on the clock.
Las Vegas, church sanctuaries, and naval ships
hang no time pieces or calendars.
They sense the sun's place
and use constellations to figure the month.

When I am on another's clock,
my central timing mechanism
wonders why I'm off schedule.
I wake at 4:00 a.m. without an alarm
and retire at 9:30 p.m. as my vision blurs.
I know how long it takes to travel without GPS.
Hypoglycemia tells me to eat,
and gastric dilatation warns me to stop.
My Muse may wake me from a nap
when it's time to fill a page.

I don't need a weather report to carry an umbrella
or bright little yellow balls on TV
to remind me to smear on sun block
and wear short sleeves.
Since pelvic radiation, I know when to pee,
and my nasal mucosa senses the pollen count.

I went Scuba diving and came up when out of air —
not when my watch told me to.
I would have been a lousy army recruit
since I stop hiking when my feet blister.
The dentist doesn't tell me when to spit,
and I know any surgery will hurt.

Left without modern devices,
humans and animals would know their places.
The sloth would hang from tree branches,
lions would chase zebras, cats would go mousing,
and my elderly dogs wouldn't leave home.

ODE TO A GRAPE

A grape grows to plumpness
without knowing its purpose or neighbors.
It doesn't appear different from the rest
but it hasn't eyes or a brain to decide
if this hanging was his destiny.

Grapes dangle in bunches on branches
sharing the same sun and showers
until harvest when all are clipped and collected
in the natural order of the grape world.
Their final destination, a smooth drink at dinner.

Some day, an individual grape may exclaim,
"Not this grape! Let me stay in the sun!
I've decided I'd rather be a raisin."

I live in suburban sprawl
where homes, spouses, children and dogs
look and act the same, have similar jobs,
and wait together to be crushed.

RANDOM ACT OF KINDNESS

My problems felt like a troubled puddle,
incapable of a clear reflection.
I called a friend and invited him out for dinner
to help me calm my ruffled waters.

I was seated on a red velveteen two-cushion couch
waiting for my guest at the Sea Grill,
a fashionable restaurant on E Street in Eureka,
and was joined by a homeless man in rough clothes,
someone I had seen outside, looking cold and tired.
He was bearded, dirty and wore scuffed work boots.
Aromas of sole, beef and corn soup drifted
over the well dressed patrons and staff.

The waitress approached him with a smile and a menu,
sat in the adjoining chair, and asked for his order.
He said he was hungry, wanted fish and beef.
She offered him a table, which he refused,
and in ten minutes she returned
from the kitchen with a broader smile
holding a full takeout dinner.
She accepted what cash he had
and said in a low voice that she noticed he had worked all day
and hoped the meal would make him feel better.
He thanked her and returned to the rainy night.

I thanked her for her behavior and with a tear
told her I appreciated her act of kindness.
Most poor people are just having a rough time
and will improve their condition with compassionate help.
The young waitress made certain his night was better,
and I had a clearer reflection of my own behavior
as former troubles now seemed minor.

ROAD TO RETIREMENT

Kneeling in my footed flannels
with mother listening,
I wasn't wishing over a rainbow
for retirement. That was what people did
when they got old like Grandpa.

I might have hinted for a bike
or a dog, which would have fallen on deaf ears,
or that Jesus would take me when I died,
but I never wished for retirement.

Years passed. I finished medical training
and my road became more directed.
I asked for divine assistance
to guide my hands and thoughts
as I cared for the sick and dying.

One day, I knew I straddled the center line
dividing must retire from should retire
so I opted out, ate from the 30 year cake,
had my picture taken, and drove home
from my hospital's retirement party.

Imagine what looks out of place:
a small puppy, tail tucked between his legs,
a child with tears without her mother,
the New York skyline in 2002,
the angle the foot takes below a fractured hip,
Richard Nixon with long hair,
Mother Teresa in tennis shorts,
and a doctor in his easy chair without a pager.

THE AMERICAN WAY OF DEATH

In America we fear death;
it is not discussed at the dinner table.
We whisper in church the very sick
are going to their final reward.
Heaven's streets are made of gold bricks
and further suffering is not allowed.
Enter the poet who makes plans
to go out with a hoot and holler,
like the fanfare of the dying calligrapher
of a Japanese death haiku.

The living give distance to the dying,
far from sight, touch or smell.
Most murmur this is an inconvenient time
to prepare for someone's funeral.
With averted eyes and shy greetings,
they ask survivors how they are feeling.
Grief will soon fall on deaf ears.

Animals show courage
by slinking away to die in private.
The shiny snake sheds skin
and slithers silently to tall grass.
A raven with a broken wing
is never seen flying away.
Elephants know where the boneyard is
and dinosaurs knew how to become oil.

Humans honor customs and rituals
planning funerals while still alive,
picking their own pall-bearers and psalms.
They make deliberate lists of who will get
their accumulated treasures.

Minnesotans decide what kind of cabbage
will be shredded and served in green jello
next to bowls of three bean salad
in the damp, mildew-laden church basement.

LIFE WAS BETTER ONCE

Mr. K was born in 1954 in Oregon,
attended high school and played football.
He was as wide as he was tall
and started as the varsity right guard
on a championship team.

Today he is 59, living in a nursing home
so he can easily be transported
for kidney failure treatments.

I was new to his life and his sad story.
He left school without a degree,
worked the lumber mill, and washed dishes at night.
He had no family money, didn't qualify for a scholarship,
and was too big for the Army.
He cleaned oil vats at the refinery,
sweltered during harvest times,
was the sole Caucasian picking strawberries and melons.
He was paid minimum wage and lived in his car.
All the while his diabetes progressed; he lost his leg
but not his girth or appetite.
Now he has to deal with a new doctor.

When he was born, I was an Eagle Scout.
When he sawed lumber, I went to medical school.
When he picked crops, I practiced Nephrology.
Now, 14 years his senior, we have little in common
except that I'm holding his medical record.

My biggest issue today was having to drive a rental,
since my SUV needed a new part before I could return
to my mansion overlooking a bay with wife and dogs.

His main concern that day was that
the nursing home would not let him eat potatoes.
I made the call and solved his only request.

It's better to peak later than too early
unless you've just invented Facebook
and can afford to drop out of school.

ODE TO THE TELEPHONE

I remember my grandfather's telephone,
the size of a pay phone in Grand Central Station,
attached to the kitchen wall of the farmhouse
with separate devices for ear and mouth.
You had to crank the handle
to call the operator,
and when Bert heard he was talking long distance
all the way from Sandstone to St.Paul,
he would stand back and shout.

In Minneapolis, city folks in the 50's
had a black dial phone, one allowed per home,
connected to a second party somewhere beyond our yard.

When too many houses had phones,
we went from Walnut 5173 to 10-5173,
and when 6 digits weren't enough,
they added area codes.
Princess phones in pastel colors
had push buttons for the dial,
with extensions in the living room,
two line houses and clever ways
of talking over a busy signal.

Later in life, I was of such worth
that I wore a beeper on my belt.
Forced to stop at a filling station's outdoor phone
was dangerous, as they were poorly lighted,
you needed change, and physicians got mugged.

When there was demand for a portable phone,
designers who offered a trunk sized transmitter

invented the 10 pound Motorola hand-held,
useful also as a weapon to fend off attackers.
Finally, my Blackberry arrived, then a smart phone,
and now wrist watches with pictures.

Now, it's hard to be out of touch with anyone.

WHAT TO DO ABOUT OLD THINGS

OLD BUILDINGS

Our church was built 45 years ago,
but congregations have swelled and shrunk.
Money was tight and we lost our outdoor lights
The Deacons voted for a quick fix,
which required an electrician as old as the belfry
and a willing assistant eager to learn and work for free.
Once rewired, refitted and lighting the night,
the fragile globes needed cleaning,
which required the touch of a surgeon,
the stamina of a cheetah,
and the temperament of a priest on drugs.

OLD HUSBANDS

Old husbands need space
to pretend they haven't aged.
If he's been blessed with a steady wife,
empty moments will leave his life.
The what-might-have-beens are gone,
sex before dinner a thing of the past.
Going to bed naked after a communal bath
now heightens the urge to putter in the garage.
To fill the void of full employment, get him an old dog.

OLD CLOTHES

Naval duty required 1 of 3 outfits be assigned daily.
Shoes and uniforms were color coordinated
to black, brown or white.
At sea, you wore work clothes;
on land, precise dress codes ruled.

In high school and college two outfits sufficed:
today's and tomorrow's.
My doctoring garb was a long white coat
worn over everything.
In surgery, we wore green scrubs
for operating on bloody people,
for dining in the cafeteria, and for sleep,
after untying and removing our shoes
but not our socks.

OLD DREAMS

My dreams have never aged, but linger
in the nocturnal lobe of my brain
and reappear during rapid eye movement sleep.
I was three and my Mother was pregnant
but let me sit down on the escalator
as we descended in a department store.
My little fingers fit nicely between the slats
but at the bottom, my hand disappeared . . .

A frightened horse bucked me off at age 12
on a narrow trail in Glacier National Park,
We both slid down the slippery shale.
He was caught by a solitary slender tree,
but I missed grabbing his halter . . .

The ice had begun to break up
in early spring on a Minnesota lake
when the driver of the speed boat hit a log.
We flipped out as the boat disappeared.
Fortunately, the bow of the craft had trapped air
so we clung to each other but were too cold to call for help.
We feebly discussed the process of drowning
but our hands were so cold, we let go . . .

I was only 26 but old enough and married enough
to think being intoxicated with a half naked classmate
might not be a wise thing to do.
We had the good sense to stop, but for years later I dreamt
she would show up for our 50th class reunion
and look as sweet as she did that night . . .

SAND DOLLARS

I was alone in a Kelp bed
60 feet under the ocean
off the coast of Bon Aire,
noted for its gentle current.

It was midnight and lobster picking was over
when I noticed hundreds of sand dollars in the shadow
made by our dive boat on anchor.

They eat during slack tide and line upright,
stuck in the sand equidistant from each other
forming perfect rows and columns
so all bellies faced in one direction

They were waiting for the current to bring them dinner
as they have no feet to fetch nor fins to swim.
I imagined they dined on the smallest of plankton
or debris left over from the recent feeding frenzy
caused by crabs, lobsters and divers.

It's a mystery how they mate
but they all look the same.
Since they have no arms or legs,
it's lucky they have no predators.

After their life cycle, they are washed ashore.
When their soft parts have dried in the sun
they end up in beach souvenir shops
adorned with barnacles,
painted in bright colors
to cover their sandy shells.

EVENING SKY

No star announced my birth.
Wise men on camels stayed home
since they had no reason to come
to midwinter Minnesota.

At age 70, I was close to my place of birth
as the evening sky was punctuated
with flashes of lightning and rolling thunder,
omens of the approaching storm.
As a child I felt the heavens were talking to me
whenever early summer storms crossed the plains.

I was the acting king of my birthdays
since it can snow, rain, hail or shine in April.
I was not crowned and wore no ermine,
but was blessed with regal thoughts of youth,
calling my Schwinn bike my chariot,
the German Shepherd next door my steed,
sharp clipping shears my weapon,
as I protected myself with the garbage can lid.

III. HOME DELIVERY

HOME DELIVERY

"Whom can I ask
what I came to make
happen in this world?"
—Pablo Neruda
El Libro de las Preguntas XXXI

The first chore I remember
was to pick crab grass from our lawn
every Saturday morning before the movies.
I moved on to delivering
the *Minneapolis Tribune*
to homes in the neighborhood
on my red Schwinn bike.

We 12-year-olds gathered at 6:00 a.m.
in the news shack to claim our stash,
dropped from the printing press truck.
We carefully counted and rolled papers,
which we stuffed into our canvas bags
and peddled like Flash Gordon
bringing news to the city.
We collected money from homeowners monthly,
going house to house alone in the evening.
Meeting our customers and their dogs
meant hope for a tip and a friendly smile.

I was the first child my mother delivered,
a 10-pound monster who prolonged labor
enough that I was never forgiven for her pain.
I delivered my first baby at a Salvation Army Home
for unwed mothers in St. Paul, Minnesota.
The girl was 16 and didn't care.
It was easy to catch the child,

propelled with a grunt and shove
into my waiting hands, alive and kicking.

As I handed him to an attending Nun,
the new mother walked out the door
and the infant was adopted the next day.

NOT SAID

"thoughts held back hold more
than those one says aloud."
       "Speech over Spilled Milk"
              — Joseph Brodsky

At night old men dream
ideas never spoken.
During the day they may regret
paths never seen or taken.

How swiftly the first half of life is over,
becoming only memories and yellowed photographs.
Once you notice muscles shrinking,
skin wrinkling and eyelids drooping,
you fear your unsteady gait and slow reflexes
will abandon you when you slip on a rug.
The quads once bulged, biceps flexed,
lungs never failed doing two stairs at a time.
Hip and shoulder joints rotated easily without pain
and you never lost your car key or forgot to eat.

An anesthesiologist hid his chest pain
while observing surgeons replacing arteries
into diseased hearts of bodies he controlled.
One day he went home and exercised on his treadmill
until his aching heart stopped
along with the hidden pain
he had harbored and ignored
for years.

DRAGONS ARE PRINCESSES WAITING TO BE KISSED

waiting
for
a kiss
a dragon
hiding
behind a tree
holds
its hot breath
settles
hunkers
stretches
sees
a blind troubador
singing
stumbling
falls face first
and kisses
hot lips
explode
a cloud
shrinks
for a
princess
who
was waiting
for a
kiss.

INVENTORY OF AN OLD HOUSE

Grandma passed after 86 years,
living alone in her yellow, weathered, peeling
farmhouse on a hill for 70 years.
As a new bride she made her bed,
filled each room with love, a succession of husbands
and loaves of freshly baked bread.

Refusing visitors or phone calls,
seldom seen in public since last widowed,
she left all the lives she'd touched
and spent her five last lonely years with her cats.

The house was in a forest,
land parceled out for grazing.
She was buried in a pauper's grave
under words from a divinity intern.
With the old recluse gone,
I was court appointed to settle the estate
and provide an inventory of the furnishings.

On a gloomy day I entered
her 5000 square foot mansion
with my teenagers, armed with flashlights.

Ghost house cobwebs thick in every corner,
dust covering ancient furniture and mirrors.
Graves for cats by weather beaten porches,
next to planters with dead geraniums.

Her dining room was a library
with stacks of *National Geographic*
ordered by date from the Eisenhower days,

side by side with Sunday editions
of the *New York Times*, all unread.

We discovered clothes arranged by decade,
labeled, bagged and stacked.
Shoes were paired, polished and sorted
with colorful tabs of their history.
Undergarments, blouses and nightclothes
were boxed by size.

Thousands of postage stamps waiting licking,
ordered by country as if planning a trip,
with travel brochures of exotic places.
A bottle cap collection was on display
in the pantry, next to a set of Liberty Head dimes.
Boxes and cans of cat food
were stuffed under the kitchen table.

No family pictures adorned her walls.
Hanging in the parlor was a Jacques Deny,
"After the Storm," worth a fortune.
Silver tea sets were arranged by marriage
and furniture spanned seven decades.

Medicine shelves bulged with tinctures
and extracts from vital organs.
All preparations contained
liberal concentrations
of alcohol and morphine.
We found racks of home dyeing kits
in her personal beauty locker,
allowing her to be any color she desired.
False teeth sets, a smiling audience
to our explorations through her closets,
seemed to approve of our visit.

We discovered one pan in her kitchen
used to boil water for eggs
for an occasional breakfast
with tea, toast and marmalade.
Several bottles of ale were stored
for a desired male visitor.

In the garage a 1940 Ford
with 1256 miles on the odometer,
flat tires and dozens of mice
using the seats for nesting.

As we finished our search, we knew
that her treasures while on earth
were not transferred to heaven.

ODE TO COYOTES AND TIMBERWOLVES

After a light rain, the early sunshine
glistens off faults in the rocks.
Our resident pack of coyotes
stretches and barks in unison.
What to do about breakfast?

The wiley coyote of comic book fame
is actually a small timberwolf
and a nuisance to farms and forests.
They like to eat babies of anything,
including the chicken hatching the egg.

Timberwolves were close to extinct
and adorned the cover of *Time*,
stirring tree huggers but not farmers
to reintroduce them to the woods,
where they thrived and began to mate
with their lesser and smaller relatives,
producing a genetically enhanced menace.

Occasionally, our neighborhood is overrun
by these critters, who are protected.
Once they've eaten all the rabbits,
they change their diets to include
cats, small dogs and raccoons.

In Texas you can shoot a threatening menace;
in Idaho you can carry a gun.
Here in California, if you dare harm
anything in the woods
you'll be arrested by Park Rangers.

Perhaps, visitors coming over our southern border
can be persuaded to change their diet
from horse meat tacos to flank of small wolf.
In the meantime, keep young children indoors.

THE SHOW WENT ON

There's nothing wrong with America
when children from the Lutheran school
of the Good Shepherd in Novato, California
can present "Guys and Dolls"
to a packed house on a rainy night.

These kids were six feet tall on stage
although none rose to my waist
in the mix of proud parents and flowers.
Listen up, next President, and reward
all the bands, theatricals, sports and orchestras
which were decimated for budgetary reasons.

What joy, this evening packed with song and dance,
with beaming smiles for performers and audience.
Large hearts were squeezed through pre-teen vocal cords.
No way this cast will ever be seen in the company of
gangs and thugs, failing grades, or bad habits.
My social security checks will never bounce
if this band of youth will be running the country.

LAMENT TO A FALLEN POET

William Butler Yeats
was *emptied of his poetry*
at the age of 74
and laid to rest under
bare Ben Bulben's head.

He died one year before I was born.
I am now that age and haven't seen
the droughts, pandemics or starvation he lived through.
I did not witness the German gas attacks
that laid populations into trenches
or the troubles of Ireland resulting in hangings.

I loved my times and driving my '57 Chevy,
flying on a 747 to London first class,
witnessing men walking on the moon,
reading *The Isle of Innisfree* in high school
and finally visiting Dublin.

Now, I am as old as that great poet
when he gathered men to his coffin
to remind them he had been transformed as
a terrible beauty was born.

Will someone read me in 74 years?
If they do, they selected poorly,
for by the year of our Lord, 2088,
if I am capable of remembering a date
and have enough of my limbs to ambulate
with eyes clouded by cataracts,
I will hobble to the autograph table
and see who survived our troubles.

AFTER THE HOUSE BURNED DOWN

You have a sweet smile and a friendly soul,
and I like how you twirl your hair around your fingers.

What is your favorite color?
My favorite color is dark grey, especially at night.

You have beautiful hair and grey green eyes.
Only one, the other got burnt.

Who is your favorite poet?
Emily Dickinson. She never left her house.

My dad died when I was young.
My mother always told me better scarred than dead.

Do you want to walk in the rain with me?
Yes, I love my hooded slicker since I look like everyone else.

May I kiss you?
Yes, if you keep both eyes closed.

ROAN GENERATORS

Our Boy Scout camp, Flaming Pine,
was rustic luxury in the woods of northern Minnesota
on Mirror Lake near Togo, population 7.
Three Roan generators supplied current
for a walk-in freezer, the mess hall, headquarters
and lights in two latrines for 70 campers.

Tent sites were scattered across 2 acres,
and we slept under the canvas
of surplus 16x16 foot WWII surplus
army issued tents.
Each platform allowed 6 spaces
for cot, foot locker and supplies.
The generators brought a restful drone
to the silence of the woods and lake.
It sounded like a mosquito swarm
without the annoying bites.

In 1953 the Rural Electrification Authority
came to town, and all temperate forests
had to be leveled 30 feet back from the dirt roads
so utility poles could be planted for power lines.

Crestview, my Grandfather's farm,
got the same service from the REA,
and suddenly, daily life and chores were easier.
Gone were gas lights and ice boxes.
Grandma Lil got a washing machine,
replacing the scrub board and wringer.
The cows were milked by gentle suction
instead of cold hands in the morning.
Soothing radio music calmed the cows,
the horses, bats, mice, cats and dog.

FAMILY SECRETS

I was 10 years old, assigned kitchen duty
as the guests left and the party ended.
Mother washed, I dried and put away.

After the family went to bed,
I dragged the short ladder out
so I could reach the upper shelf
reserved for the good china plates and cups.

Behind stacked dishes, I found a space
that my small hand had never explored
because I was not allowed to search
closed drawers, closets or top shelves.

Way in the back, behind dainty china cups,
I found 2 packs of Lucky Strikes, one opened,
a Zippo lighter, a half pint of Korbel spiced brandy,
and a stack of 5 dollar bills, held by a rubber band.
I discovered a packet of something with a French logo,
a stub from an afternoon matinee,
and a tin of Sen-Sens.

Growing up in the 50's, I heard gossip
that women were destined to be housewives,
serve their Creator, propagate,
and always obey their husbands.
They were on earth to raise children
and never wonder or wander.

Here on the shelf, I discovered my Mother's secrets.
Mom? . . . who supervised brushing of teeth,
heard our prayers, dressed us for Sunday School,
put rollers in her hair at night and toned down her make-up —
here was another life.

I had seen pictures of lacy underwear
in catalogues at the caddy shack
and was curious what went on behind my parents' bedroom door.
When next they slipped inside at night,
I listened through the wall
with my mail order stethoscope.

CLEAN DESK, CLEAN MIND

My desktop must be clean before I write,
swept clear of images from heart and past.
I sit and call my muse to stop her flight.

Now, armed with pen and pad, I start
to let a stream of words flow brain to breast.
My desktop must be clean before I write.

Soon words are hunting others with delight
to link with those whose lucky charm will last.
I sit and call my muse to stop her flight.

I'm lost in time as day fades into night.
I taste my words becoming rising yeast.
My desktop must be clean before I write.

This poem needs polish to be right,
then, blessed, I lift it off my heaving chest.
I call my muse to stop at once her flight.

It's time to bring the words into the light;
like Mary bringing Jesus to the world.
I'm blessed with editors and friends
who help illuminate images of words.
My desktop must be clean before I write.

I beckon my muse to start another flight.

SUPER BOWL 50

Tonight, Macy's fired off Super Bowl season
at the Ferry Building on Market Street
before crowds who flocked to watch
grown men set off firecrackers.

This incendiary display was delivered live
on Channel 5, but I, living across the bay,
saw it a tenth of a second quicker from my deck.

This deck, one of 7 at my house,
will soon belong to Mr. and Mrs. Hastings,
who are moving from Boston
to be nearer their grandchildren.
They'll love the water and the view
of Angel Island, tall ships and pelicans.
Lucky for me, they have dough.

Super Bowl has always been overplayed,
but it's just another football game
unless, of course, the 49ers win.
Few cities have been blessed
with world champions in the big three events
of football, baseball and basketball.

Now, it is time to downsize expectations
and let Detroit win something
since it's bad enough to be from there.

Everyone will watch highly paid gladiators
commit mayhem without killing.
If Donald Trump wins the hot political race,
a new Nero might change the ending.

WHY ASK?

"Sometimes you have to live
at the edge of your questions."
from *Blackberries in the Dream House*
—Diane Frank

I never questioned authority
and obeyed the Boy Scout laws
so was alarmed to learn
40% of American males have been arrested
for petty theft, burglaries, drug possession
and violence by age 23.

I question why it wasn't me?
I question why I married at age 22?
I wonder how it might have been
if my home town had been bombed like London
or flooded like New Orleans?

But since I'm here and healthy,
years past the age when most die,
I need to question what I'm doing
with these extra years?

I'm not altruistic enough
to volunteer to fight Ebola in Liberia
or generous enough
to let a homeless man live with me.
I pass by sidewalk charity requests
and ignore people with a Watchtower.
I don't fill the pail next to a ringing Santa
or drop spare change into the church platter.

I have retired my stethoscope and pager,
and won't be bothered if Social Security defaults.
I question the need for 8 hours of sleep,
and doubt the truth of news on TV.
I still fish but release them back to the river.
I haven't run the Bay to Breakers for years,
but I walk the dogs and do my chores.
I am friendly towards my neighbors
and tip the postwoman and scavengers
when I remember the Christmas spirit.

IV. COURTING AT THE STRAWBERRY

COURTING AT THE STRAWBERRY

Single and alone, Canada geese
flew into the strawberry pasture
thirty minutes before the spring equinox.
The larger males hissed and lunged
at other males and then each selected
a solitary female, who was coyly observing
but fluffing feathers and making cooing noises.
They paired up without exchanging
phone numbers or next of kin.

The male strutted; she primped;
and with a tangling of necks
walked off a few paces, so others
would declare them a couple —
all done without documents
or a church choir and organ.

I'm told geese mate for life,
until they fly over a rice field
loaded with hungry hunters
before Christmas.

HOT POTATOES

Dr. Crapper invented the flush toilet
while people still used latrines,
poorly dug holes in the ground
common in Turkey and China.
Toilet tissues came much later,
but folks still warmed their feet with hot potatoes.

On our family farm in Minnesota, breakfast was potatoes
from bed and cooked with eggs near the toilet.
Following the meal and dishes, we looked later
for tissues and a path to the 4 hole latrine.
The toilet, made for Grandma, was china,
when she feared walking on frozen ground.

Morning meant urging animals from nests in the ground,
feeding pigs with leftover scraps and potatoes,
milking cows, washing company dishes, like china,
for the minister and his wife. When they visited, the toilet
was reserved for them, and the family agreed to use the latrine.
We were much happier after they went home later.

Children played canasta, the organ and later
bobbed for apples picked off the ground.
We took turns in line at the latrine,
then hurried back to heat the night's potatoes
so all could warm their feet near the toilet
which was close to a large map of China.

Everyone had to memorize it: China,
Russia, Mongolia, Tibet and later
we'd dream of far away places without toilets
where people slept outdoors on the ground,
ate rice and barley, but not potatoes,
and used the river as their latrine.

Our river was drinking water and not a latrine,
so things must be different when you visit China.
Pictures of Chinese eyes seemed like a potato's
head, which we decorated with raisins and corn. Later
we ate the whole thing with beef and pork, freshly ground.
Happily, we all got a chance to use the indoor toilet.

The latrine was torn down and replaced later.
We didn't go to China or sleep on the ground,
and all our potatoes seemed shaped like a toilet.

SEAHORSES IN SOFT CORAL

1. Steady Light

Enchanting my field of vision
200 feet below sea level,
was a 6 foot spiral of broad leaved
soft coral awash with flecks of red,
swaying gently in the mild current
and the home for a colony of seahorses.

Fathers were loaded with tiny infants
from their sudden retching for delivery
as mothers nibbled soft coral leaves.
Teenagers looked for those of the opposite sex,
having grown rapidly after birth
pretending they were lookouts for danger.
As my air supply dropped, I sadly left
this utopia on the ocean floor.

2. Leap to Justice

Pete and I were diving off Klein Bonaire
in the crystal clear water of the Dutch Antilles
at the Equator in July, avoiding the heat.
Pete, a blood-seeking diver from California,
spotted a colony of seahorses in the coral.
He armed his spear gun hoping to kill
a half-dozen of the tiny creatures
when a Barracuda guarding the colony
snipped off part of the invader's ear.

We had to ascend to find a doctor,
and the seahorses remained intact.

A MINNESOTA LIST POEM

Coming from the Midwest to be educated,
I attended an Ivy League college near Boston
and in my spare time, played hockey
My new friends were like other 18 year olds,
except their relatives had come over on the Mayflower.
Mine had come later in steerage and moved west.

I told my new roommates I would be honored
to enlighten them on what goes on beyond Ohio.
Minnesota has 10,000 lakes with names,
and the mosquito is the state bird.
It is full of Scandinavians, many not plugged into the grid
but we have paved roads and telephone poles.
We eat fish soaked in lye and boiled in milk.
We don't play lacrosse with Indians
but we skate outdoors, starting in November.

In January, it is 50 degrees below
and in July, 120 degrees above.
It snows 8 months a year; then the Mississippi floods.
Our airport handles DC3s, and several counties
allow one cow per family in the back yard for milk.

We make friends with our pets:
goats, pigs, sheep and chickens
before we kill them for dinner.
We don't eat foreign food or drink wine.
When entertaining we serve coffee, pickled herring,
bean filled Jello molds, head cheese, beer and potatoes.

They listened and took notes
since they were scholarly
but as the coach dropped the puck,
we were all on the same team.

TATTOOS

Only sailors on drunken leave
in a country with a king,
where tattoo parlors thrive
and booze is cheap,
end up with a naked lady
with fake blood and a large bust
covering a major portion of their chest

Horses are tattooed on their upper lip;
cows are branded on their flank.
Maori warriors of New Zealand,
notorious for macabre facial contortions,
covered their bodies with such inky renditions
of fauna, flora and battle scenes,
invading armies fled their shores.

Better to leave markings to painters
and leave your skin clean.
A tattoo of *MARY FOREVER* will not
make *SALLY* merry when you fall in love
and plan to marry.

BRIEF IMPRESSIONS

1.
In the one second passing
I could see
     her left hand
on the grey steering wheel
head bobbing to an iPod,
     her right hand holding a smart phone,
occasionally glancing
     over her shoulder
        at her child
           in an infant seat
     near the large dog
        behind her.
She missed the switch from amber to red
and in the crosswalk struck a wheelchair
with a paraplegic veteran from Afghanistan
who was trying to avoid the collision with hand controls.

2.
I was home on leave from the Navy
with orders to report to Norfolk, Virginia in two days
for an extended cruise on the USS Columbus,
which meant Southeast Asia was certain.

I was leaving a darkened restaurant with my first wife
during a Minnesota snow storm which blinded my vision,
so I failed to notice a car coming from my left.
It was in the parking lane and not the street lane
as it suddenly tore off my front bumper.

The driver was uninjured, as were we,
but there were no phones.
As I drove to find one, I ran a red light
and forced a driver into snow.

A State trooper pulled me over
and asked if I had a really good excuse
for my behavior
or would I like to spend the night in jail?

I told him my companion was my soon to be ex-wife.
We had dinner with her new boyfriend;
my car was smashed by a drunken school teacher;
and I'm colorblind and didn't see
the light through all the snow.

I said my ship will probably take me to Vietnam.
He said he felt sorry for me and offered to take me home.

EIGHT DEADLY SINS

I obeyed my mother when she requested
one loaf of white bread sliced at the market.
Three blocks later I remembered
she wanted tongue and liver, if it was free.
I'm no Glutton and disgusted by the choices
said they were out.

I didn't win merit badge #36,
so I couldn't add the golden palm
to my Eagle Badge ribbon.
I rejected promotion to Lieutenant Commander in the Navy
and refused advancement to Clinical Professor of Medicine,
so I wasn't always full of Pride.

I chased after women
between my marriages to two lovely ladies,
so wasn't Jealous when other men Lusted after them.

I didn't Envy anyone in a red Ferrari
since I couldn't get into or out of such a small car.
No Avarice for me; I made plenty of money.

I waken early, exercise frequently, eat modestly,
walked every day with all my dogs.
I admire the Sloth, smart enough to live in trees near food.

I am not Angry with my Sister who is angered
with our Nephew since he married a he.
Is being Gay the 8th?

CYCLE OF LIFE

My grandfather planted wheat,
after threshing collected oats,
which he sent to a mill
to become flour for bread.

The cast iron stove fueled with kindling,
potatoes from the field,
eggs from chickens,
bacon from a pig,
milk and cream from cows
became breakfast.

Coffee brewed,
bread toasted and spread
with headcheese from pigs
fed 13 mouths
for 70 years
without plumbing
without electricity
without hospitals

and the dumpling stew
was delicious.

THE NOTHINGMAN

The nothingman
can write a something poem
if his once-in-a-while mind
will move the furniture around,
paint walls, spread fresh sheets
and let the poem move in
to share a bed and a meal,
maybe even the bathroom.

Mind, tell body to feed the poem;
don't let it linger on your tongue.
Let the poem wake up early
and after stretching,
be free to write about nothingness.
The poem about lucky words
flying randomly in the cranial cavern
the mind occupies will emerge.

I watch my aging dogs
shape their own destinies —
one without teeth to chew,
the other with arthritic hips.
Left alone, they would flounder.
If we appreciate our nothingness,
we have no boundaries but universal wisdom.

Don't pick a fight with someone bigger
or spoil the day for someone younger.
Make your last thought at night:
"Did I add today to my spiritual light?"

BARK WORSE THAN BITE

My former neighbor complained
to his real estate broker
about a liability next door:
"my neighbor has two barking dogs."

Of course they bark, not being able
to shout, whistle or use sign language.
When people or pets pass near the balcony,
my dogs courageously guard their castle.

I've considered buying a dragon
to monitor the easement
and found a web site selling
mythological creatures from Camelot.

The trouble with dragons,
which probably led to their extinction,
became painfully clear to early handlers.
They couldn't be trained not to eat their owner.
They shoot out disgusting sulfuric fumes
which stink up the neighborhood
and burn down homes and forests.

If a neighbor complains about my Bichons again,
I'll buy cockroaches, infest his kitchen,
and blame it all on a faulty sewer drain.

MONTEREY LIGHTHOUSE

The widow's walk in the lighthouse
serves double duty. On stormy nights
it shines a beam for homebound ships,
and in the morning allows a woman
a solitary place to pace and worry,
searching for her captain's ship
on the horizon.

She stares through morning haze,
scanning Monterey Bay
with hopes to sight the tip of a mast
or the distinctive bulge of her husband's ship.

Disappointed, she returns to her bed
and dreams the worst seafaring tales —
ships dashed on rocks, men in lifeboats,
pieces of a splintered hull.

Awakening drenched in sweat,
she sees nothing but shadows,
imagined forms tossed by waves
higher than the tallest mast
of any ship she knows.

Friends and kin gather at the base
of the Monterey Lighthouse
to hold a vigil.

EATING LILY PADS

Lily pads make lovely paintings,
floating on a mountain lake
with clouds and pine trees casting shadows
on large green leaves from submerged roots
blending with the shoreline growth.

I've watched Alaskan moose
knee deep with noses busy
shoveling quantities of food
into cavernous mouths
with extra for the calf.

A moose must be within
one mile of fresh water to survive.
Roads and buildings have buried trails
which once guided them to food.
While flying over tundra in a small plane,
I've seen great herds of moose migrating
and I wondered if they could find
a lake big enough for all to have a drink.

THE SECRET LIVES OF WAVES

I listen to waves breaking on the beach
below the cliff where I lived for 18 years
and wondered who else was hearing their song?

Is someone in Tonga listening?
Their wave song may be clashing cymbals,
forewarning them of an impending storm.
A giant wave in Hawaii is tantamount
to victory for the long war canoes.
Ships in harbor time their departures
while reading waves and tides.

Can we alter the pitch and eavesdrop
on what other listeners are thinking
as we share waves lulling us to sleep?
I dream of free running striped bass,
which I followed as they rode the wave.

I shout into wind and rain as I cast
but strip off clothes under a warm sun.
I've talked to snow drifts as I marched to school
and thanked barrier reefs for protecting
a delicate shoreline with wrack for birds.

Waves achieve monstrous heights
when the moon is rising from the eastern sky
and once clearing Mt. Tam,
I know that Ocean beach
is being bashed by frisky waves
recently born over the horizon
after a typhoon struck the Azures.

MILKING

At 4:00 a.m.
in the still of a Minnesota winter
careful to not disturb his wife and four young children,
Grandfather Wahlberg would rise from a warm bed
to cold clothes,
tramp a new path through snow from kitchen to barn,
and smell sixteen Holstein cows
with filled udders, empty bowels and stomachs.

They would turn their heads religiously
half to the left, half to the right,
waiting for their oats and hay
and his cold hands on washed teats.

He named each of his herd
when it dropped its first calf
and joined the army of patient providers
of dairy fresh milk for city folks.

The fresh, unpasteurized whole milk
was stored in five gallon cans in a cold stream
until the cream rose to the top and was skimmed off
to be sold to creameries for ice cream and cheese.

Grandpa would let us drink fresh from the cow
so we stood close to the udder with mouths open.
He would squirt a full stream of warmth towards our faces,
onto our tongues and do the same for barn cats
waiting their turn.

We city kids on the farm for a month
developed a personal relationship with the cows,
but our mothers wouldn't let us take one home.

OUT FOR A STROLL

A solitary grey haired man
is not a suspect of interest
if attached to leashes and following
small, white, well-mannered canines.

When I walk my dogs on the Loch Lomond boardwalk
bordering the San Rafael Bay,
we frequently pass other attached humans
who slack leashes if all dogs
have upturned tails.

The dogs now perform a ritual dance
to a symphony in a high pitch
only they can hear.

In this self-conducted orchestra,
the alpha dogs are basses,
and the timid ones are winds.
The first bass enters with a growl
while the winds scurry in treble clef,
not certain of the motive or key.

When kettle drums are sensed
and French horns wail forest sounds,
the dogs supply a cacophony of sniffing:
nose to nose, nose to butt, nose to ears
and back to a lot of butt in the final score.

Suddenly, the alpha mutt tugs
to be unrestrained from his human
so all dogs can venture into bushes
and decide on mating partners
or at least find a good place to squat.

A triangle calls them back to eat.

POETRY PIZZA

Poetry becomes an expression that
filters into the world slowly.
—Robert Hass

Dark was the name given to the times
when houses were little more than caves
and the only joys in the peasant's life
were food, song, fire and fellowship.
Troubadours would sing magic lyrics,
passing news and music to people
huddled around the central fire,
cooking and eating pizza and washing it down
with a suspect brew from grapes crushed last year.

I like to catch an idea as it tumbles
like a tornado before it somersaults
and crumples into dust and disappears.
If I've eaten a pepperoni and garlic pizza,
I keep a note pad at my bedside
to jot down flashy tidbits from gastric dreams
that may or may not make sense in the morning.

Since poetry has such an irresistible pull
on our emotions and life,
it remains a force of enlightenment,
surviving to this day.

THE SPICE OF LIFE

I grew up in a Swedish kitchen
where pepper was exotic.
Most of what we ate was white —
Wonder bread, mashed potatoes,
cream based sauces and whole milk.

In college in Boston
I was served mutton stew,
spinach salad and brussel sprouts.
We drank flavored teas, ate crunchy buns
and had flaming things for dessert.

Thanksgiving, we had Maine lobsters.
For Christmas, hasty pudding was served.
Instead of bananas, we ate figs,
and I tasted real Italian sausage.

In Paris, I ate rabbit; in Marseilles, octopus.
In Baja, the taco meat was either horse or dog.
Turtle was delicious in Hawaii
and goat savory in Bon Aire.
The most tender meat was moose in Canada.

After 45 years of eating in hospitals,
I've grown accustomed to anything
warm and filling after midnight.
Fortunately, I was married to a woman
who besides being beautiful was a gourmet cook.
I've disappointed her since I'm not a gourmand,
being more mindful of my waist than my palate.

Now, I live in a studio apartment and eat sushi.

MY IMAGINARY VILLAGE

When I was 9 years old,
I had a village of imagination
where I was alone and could play
with all the inhabitants of my mind.
I was the Sheriff, tended bar at my hotel,
picked a posse to catch bank robbers.

I had a beautiful Queen with long blond hair
and a dog like Tom Mix's Tony.
He sat with me
on a sturdy elm tree limb
where we held court.

My home was in a tunnel
and I'd capture pet frogs for bait.
If I caught a fish, it was Moby Dick
who had just crashed into Ahab.

I made stew from carrots and peas
and when I whistled,
birds flocked to my hands.
I built a tent under the covers of my bed
and read each night with my Roy Rogers flashlight.
I made a navy from sticks
and fired rubber bands at the Brits.
I always had my unseen friend to talk with,
and he was always happy to listen
as I walked the seven blocks to and from school.

In winter, I'd skate alone
and dive into snowbanks to stop.
I was happy during childhood pretending,
and was saddened when I grew older
and found out adults always kept score.

JEREMIAH O'BRIEN

Two veterans of the sea,
one a Merchant Marine, the other
doctor to a squadron of Naval destroyers,
stood in awe at the magnificence
of the Jeremiah O'Brien,
moored at Pier 45 in San Francisco
next to a WWII submarine.

The O'Brien was a Liberty Ship,
recently outfitted to sail from port to Normandy
to celebrate the assault that ended the Second World War.
Liberty ships carried cargo and men
between home and foreign ports.
They were guarded by destroyers during transit
because of the threat of submarines.
In 1945 they brought war brides to America.

We boarded early before the tourists
and had the ship to ourselves.
We had already inspected the sub next door,
found those quarters cramped and stuffy.

But here on a cargo ship,
it was all space and hatches.
Bunks were wide, overheads tall,
tables secured to the deck.
There was a closet and chair for every sailor.

We left that day wanting to re-up
but were too old for sea duty.
Soon, we received an invitation
requesting our presence on a voyage

of the Jeremiah O'Brien during Fleet Week.
We helped secure lines, set sail, ate hot-dogs,
and were buzzed by the Blue Angels.

The ship received a cannon tribute as it sailed
under the Golden Gate Bridge with full colors flying.

ABOUT THE AUTHOR

David Connor is a retired physician living in Petaluma, California. His interest in poetry began early in life, influenced by his mother and a great aunt, a poet of the 1930's. He did not have a literary education; instead he graduated from Harvard University with a B.A. in Economics and from the University of Minnesota with a B.S. and an M.D. He practiced Nephrology in the San Francisco Bay Area for 30 years and began attending poetry workshops with Diane Frank, Dale Biron, and Prartho Sereno. In his retirement, he writes a poem every day and has traded his medical practice for fly fishing rivers. He also has a collection of signed books published by some of the most famous poets of his generation.

www.ingramcontent.com/pod-product-compliance
Lightning Source LLC
Chambersburg PA
CBHW032021090426
42741CB00006B/696